Mr St an Painted Tiger

ROBIN MELLOR

Illustrated by Lesley Harker

OXFORD
UNIVERSITY PRESS

OXFORD
UNIVERSITY PRESS

Great Clarendon Street, Oxford OX2 6DP

Oxford University Press is a department of the University of Oxford.
It furthers the University's objective of excellence in research, scholarship,
and education by publishing worldwide in

Oxford   New York

Auckland   Cape Town   Dar es Salaam   Hong Kong   Karachi
Kuala Lumpur   Madrid   Melbourne   Mexico City   Nairobi
New Delhi   Shanghai   Taipei   Toronto

With offices in

Argentina   Austria   Brazil   Chile   Czech Republic   France   Greece
Guatemala   Hungary   Italy   Japan   Poland   Portugal   Singapore
South Korea   Switzerland   Thailand   Turkey   Ukraine   Vietnam

Oxford is a registered trade mark of Oxford University Press
in the UK and in certain other countries

British Library Cataloguing in Publication Data
Data available

ISBN 978-0-19-917956-5

7 9 10 8

Available in packs
Stage 10 Pack of 6:
ISBN 978-0-19-917954-1
Stage 10 Class Pack:
ISBN 978-0-19-917960-2
Guided Reading Cards also available:
ISBN 978-0-19-917962-6

Cover artwork by Lesley Harker

Printed in China by Imago

1

Nothing ever happened in Rivermead flats. Ravi, Yasmin and Peter sat on the wall in front of the flats.

Every morning Mrs Saki took her dog for a walk. Every morning Mr Walker came out of his door, looked at the sky, and went in again. Every day the milkman came. None of them took any notice of the three children.

'Nothing ever happens,' moaned
Ravi.

Peter looked up.

'Wait a minute,' he said, 'something
is happening.'

A small blue van was stopping
outside the flats. The children watched
as a man got out. He went to the back
of the van and opened the doors.
The van was piled high with bags
and boxes.

'Someone's moving in,' said
Yasmin.

They watched as the man lifted
boxes out of the van. He looked
exciting. He wore a long purple cloak
with silver stars. Each of the boxes
had writing on the side.

Mr Stofflees looked round and saw the children. 'What's in these boxes?' asked Peter.

Mr Stofflees just smiled.

The children wanted to stay, but Peter's dad was calling. 'Time for lunch,' he said.

After lunch Ravi, Yasmin and Peter came back to the front of the flats. But the van had gone. They looked everywhere for Mr Stofflees. There was no sign of him.

'We'll see him again tomorrow,' said Yasmin.

But the next morning they couldn't find Mr Stofflees. They searched and searched. At last they went to the top of the stairs on the first floor. There was Mr Stofflees. He was painting the wall.

Ravi, Yasmin and Peter stood and watched.

First he painted a large white square. He used a large brush. When the white paint was dry he picked up a thin brush. He dipped it in the black paint and he started to draw an outline.

'What's it going to be?' Peter asked.

Mr Stofflees just smiled.

'It's a horse,' said Yasmin.

'No,' said Peter, 'it's a lion.'

'I think it's a giraffe,' said Ravi.

Yasmin shrugged. Perhaps it's not
an animal at all.

Suddenly Ravi said, 'I know. It's
a tiger.'

'Yes,' said Mr Stofflees.

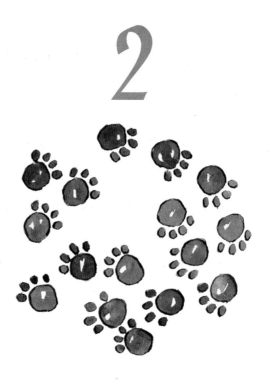

Mr Stofflees carefully drew the head, the nose, the eyes, the mouth, the whiskers, the body and, last of all – the tail.

He wiped the sweat from his face.

'I've got to let it dry now,' he said. 'Then I'll add the colour.'

Ravi, Yasmin and Peter had to go.

'Never mind,' said Mr Stofflees. 'You can come and see it tomorrow. It will be finished by then.'

Next morning Mr Stofflees got up early. He put on the colour. 'Now I'll let the paint dry,' he said to himself. Then he went out.

As soon as they had eaten breakfast, Ravi, Yasmin and Peter came to see the painting.

The children stood in front of the picture.

After a few minutes Peter said, 'It's a good painting. It looks like a real tiger.'

'Yes,' said Yasmin, 'but I've never seen a tiger that colour before.'

'No,' said Ravi. 'But apart from that it looks like a real tiger. Its eyes look very real.'

The tiger blinked and turned its eyes to look at them.

'And that mouth looks real,' said Peter.

The tiger twitched its whiskers and opened its mouth.

'You're right,' said Yasmin. 'It looks real enough to come to life.'

The tiger waved its tail, stretched its legs and slowly stepped out of the painting.

The children stepped back and stared.

The tiger looked around and sniffed the air. Then it turned and ran up the stairs.

'It's going upstairs!' Peter shouted. 'Come on. Let's follow it.'

The children ran up the stairs after
the tiger.

On the second floor Mr Singh opened
his door to take in the milk. He watched
in amazement as the tiger knocked over
a bottle with its paw.

Then it started to drink the spilt milk.

'Goodness,' said Mr Singh. 'I've never seen a tiger that colour before.'

The tiger finished the milk. It sniffed the air again and ran downstairs. The children followed.

When it got outside the tiger started
walking towards the shops. Two workmen
had been mending a hole in the road.
Now they were sitting on a wall eating
some sandwiches. The tiger took a
sandwich from one of the workmen.
It ate the sandwich. Then it ate all the
sandwiches in his lunch box. Then it ate
the lunch box.

'D'you see that?' said one of the workmen. 'My lunch box!'

The other workman just shook his head. 'I've never seen a tiger that colour before,' he said.

The tiger started off again towards the shops. When it reached the corner the tiger sat down in the middle of the road. A number 6 bus couldn't get past.

The driver lifted her cap and scratched her head. 'I've never seen a tiger that colour before,' she said.

Some of the passengers shouted at the tiger. 'Come on! Move!'

The tiger took no notice of them. In the end the bus driver tooted the horn and the tiger moved out of the way.

One of the passengers was a teacher from the school. 'This is interesting,' she said. 'I shall write to the newspapers about it.'

An old lady was walking
her little dog.

The dog started to bark when it saw
the tiger. It pulled at the lead and
wanted to play. The tiger stopped. It
looked at the dog, lifted its head and
said, 'ROARRRRRR.'

The dog hid under the old lady's
skirt.

'Well, well, well,' said the old lady.
'I've never seen a tiger that colour
before.'

In the middle of the square the Town
Council had planted a large bed of
pretty flowers. The tiger walked slowly
onto the flower bed. It rolled on its
back in the middle of the flowers and
stuck its four legs straight up in the air.
Then the tiger closed its eyes and made
a loud purring noise.

By now all the shopkeepers had
seen the tiger rolling in the flower bed.
They all came out of their shops to look
at what was going on.

'We've never seen a tiger that colour
before,' they all said. 'It can't stay
there. It will be bad for trade. We can't
have customers being scared by a
funny-coloured tiger.'

Someone sent for the police. The
policemen came and looked at the
tiger. One of them spoke into his radio.
'It's a tiger,' he said. 'But I've never
seen one that colour before.'

The policemen and the shopkeepers
were trying to decide what to do about
the tiger, when Mr Stofflees came
around the corner.

'What's going on?' he asked Ravi,
Yasmin and Peter.

'It's your tiger,' they said. 'It's come
alive. And it drank Mr Singh's milk, ate
a workman's sandwiches, stopped a bus,
frightened a dog and now it's rolling in
the flower bed.'

Mr Stofflees looked worried. 'Oh dear.
That's bad. I'll try to sort it out.'

He went over to the tiger and
whispered in its ear.

The tiger stood up and followed Mr
Stofflees. The children followed them.
They went across the square, along the
road, back to Rivermead flats and up
the stairs.

Mr Stofflees patted the tiger on the
head and tickled it under the chin. He
pointed at the empty white square.

'Now,' he said in a firm voice. 'Back
on the wall.'

The tiger growled softly, waved its tail, bent its legs and jumped back into the picture.

Mr Stofflees rubbed his hands. 'There. That should be that.'

'Mr Stofflees,' Ravi asked, 'will the tiger come off the wall again?'

'And will it eat someone?' Peter asked.

Mr Stofflees shook his head.

'Don't worry. It'll stay safe in the painting now.'

Next morning the children got up early and said, 'I wonder what will happen today?'

After breakfast they went to look for Mr Stofflees. They found him looking at the wall at the top of the stairs on the second floor.

He smiled at them.

'Hello,' he said. 'What shall I paint today?'

'A lion,' said Peter.

'No,' said Ravi. 'A cheetah.'

Yasmin thought for a moment. 'My favourite animal is an elephant but if that comes alive…'

Mr Stofflees picked up a paintbrush and smiled again.

'Very well. An elephant it shall be.'

About the author

Sometimes stories just come to me, like *Mr Stofflees*, although to be truthful, it was the idea of the tiger that came to me first. Sometimes I have to work on my stories for a long time.

I live with my family and a crazy dog called Jackie who likes to sit on my papers – and a toy orang-utan called Dexter who travels round to schools with me.